The Shipwright's Trade

THE
SHIPWRIGHT'S TRADE

Rudyard Kipling

with wood & linocuts by
James Dodds

1990
Jardine Press

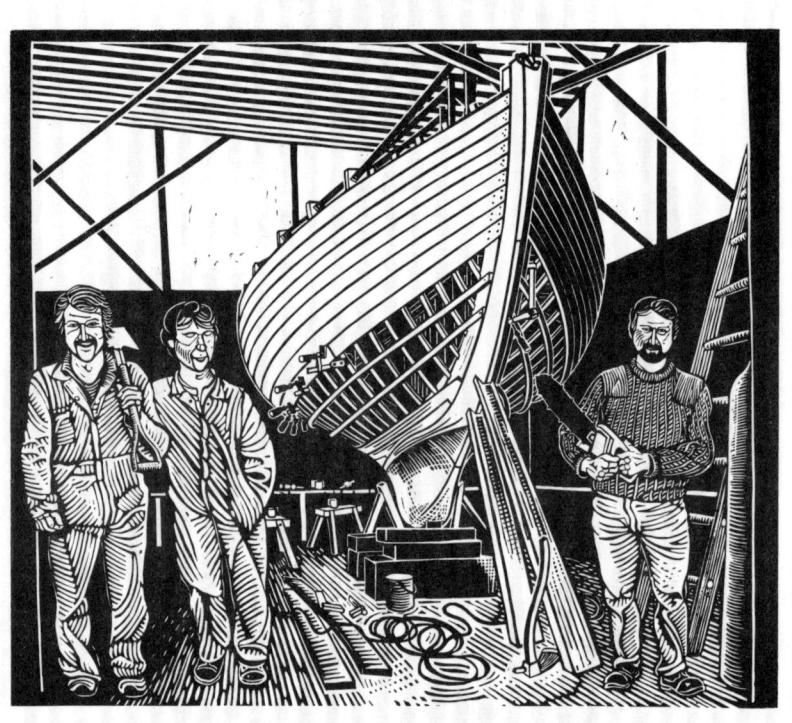

Jamie, as yet, I trust, does not identify with Noah but the nostalgia engendered by Kipling's poem has given him the opportunity to present this selection of linocuts which all relate to a period in his past.

Kipling drew his inspiration from the workaday aspect of ships and the sea, but remained a detached observer. The pictorial artist, who has earned a living from an occupation that now provides subject matter, has the advantage of technical understanding and is perhaps able to avoid a romantic image.

Jamie served his time in the shipwright's trade at a yard where Noah would have felt entirely at home. The business was established in Maldon for wooden barge building in 1894 (the year Kipling wrote his notable maritime poem 'The Mary Gloster') and continues to the present day with the re-building and re-rigging of sailing barges.

Apprentices learnt how to use the adze and other hand tools as old as the Ark. They had to suffer being watched by old men, some knowledgeable who are the most infuriating, but mostly by those who would just comment, 'you don't see this sort of work anymore'.

Jamie, even after all these years, is probably happier with the label 'ex-shipwright' than 'artist', but he knows, and this is what may produce the nostalgia, that there is no going back.

D. J. Patient B.A. Shipwright   Maldon, Essex 1990

This poem is the second part of 'The Truthful Song', first published in 1910 in the children's book 'Rewards & Fairies'. The poem brings back feelings of my own youth spent in and around a labyrinth of lean-to boat-sheds, barges, blocks and spars, learning a trade that has changed little since the building of the Ark.

Themes associated with these memories have filtered through my work for many years. This collection of eight images spans a five year period, beginning life as individual paintings and later becoming wood and linocuts. The book provides an opportunity for the images to create their own narrative.

James Dodds Shipwright M.A. (RCA)

 ' I tell this tale, which is stricter true,

Just by way of convincing you

How very little since things was made

Things have altered in the shipwright's trade.'

 In Blackwall Basin yesterday

A China barque re-fitting lay;

When a fat old man with snow-white hair

Came up to watch us working there.

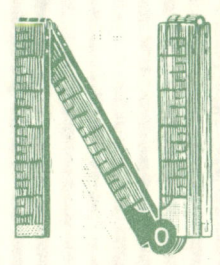Now there wasn't a knot which the riggers knew

But the old man made it - and better too ;

Nor there wasn't a sheet, or a lift, or a brace,

But the old man knew its lead and place.

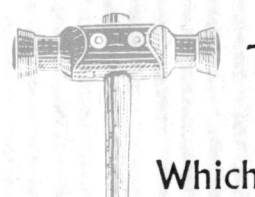 Then up and spake the caulkyers bold,

Which was packing the pump in the after-hold :

'Since you with us have made so free,

Will you kindly tell what your name might be ? '

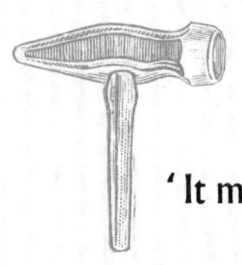

The old man kindly answered them :

' It might be Japhet, it might be Shem,

Or it might be Ham (though his skin was dark),

Whereas it is Noah, commanding the Ark. '

'Your wheel is new and your pumps are strange,

But otherwise I perceive no change,

And in less than a week, if she did not ground,

I'd sail this hooker the wide world round!'

'We tell these tales, which are strictest true,

Just by way of convincing you

How very little since things was made

Things have altered in the shipwright's trade.'

WOOD & LINOCUTS

Jardine Press Stoke By Nayland
Suffolk CO6 4SD England
ISBN: 0 9509270 4 X